Original title: 101 STRANGE BUT TRUE TENNIS FACTS.

©101 STRANGE BUT TRUE TENNIS FACTS, Carlos Martínez Cerdá y Víctor Martínez Cerdá, 2023

© Cover and illustrations: V&C Brothers
Proofreading: V&C Brothers

Writers: Víctor Martínez Cerdá and Carlos Martínez Cerdá (V&C Brothers)

Layout and design: V&C Brothers

All rights reserved. No part of this publication may be reproduced, stored in a retrieval system or transmitted in any form or by any means, mechanical, photochemical, electronic, magnetic, electro-optical, photocopying, information retrieval system, or otherwise, now or in the future, without the prior written permission of the copyright holders.

101
STRANGE BUT TRUE
TENNIS FACTS

1

Most historians believe that tennis originated in the monastic cloisters in northern France in the 12th century, where a game known as "jeu de paume" or "game of the palm" was played.

This game involved hitting a ball with the bare hand against a wall and became popular among the French nobility.

It wasn't until the 16th century that rackets came into use, allowing for greater control and precision in hitting the ball. As the game evolved, it began to be called "tennis" and became popular in both England and France.

King Henry VIII of England was a big fan of the game and played on a special court at Hampton Court Palace known as the royal tennis court.

Tennis became an Olympic sport in 1896 and has been part of the Summer Olympics ever since, with the exception of the 1904 Games.

Currently, it is one of the most popular and widely played sports in the world, with numerous professional tournaments and a large number of amateur players.

2

Samuel Groth is an Australian tennis player who is known for having one of the fastest serves in the history of tennis.

At the ATP Challenger in Busan in 2012, Groth hit a blistering serve at an incredible speed of 263 kilometers per hour (163.7 miles per hour), becoming the fastest recorded serve in the history of tennis.

This serve surpassed the previous record held by Croatian player Ivo Karlovic, who had achieved a serve of 251 kilometers per hour in a Davis Cup match in 2011.

Groth's serve was so fast that his opponent barely had time to react and it became an "ace", an unstoppable serve that cannot be returned.

Groth has been recognized as one of the players with the fastest serves on the professional circuit.

His average serve speed is around 220 kilometers per hour, making him one of the most feared players in service confrontations.

Although Groth never reached the top of the world rankings, his powerful serve allowed him to win several Challenger tournaments and have outstanding performances in Grand Slams.

His serve is considered one of the deadliest weapons in modern tennis, and remains a benchmark in the sport for any player aspiring to have an equally powerful serve.

3

Although tennis is considered a sport for the elites, in reality tennis players' salaries are not as exorbitant as those of basketball or football players.

An average tennis player can earn up to $220,611 per year.

That's quite a bit of money, but compared to the average NBA player's earnings of $7.7 million per year, it's a relatively small amount.

However, when we talk about tennis celebrities, we do see juicy sums of money.

A good example is the Spanish tennis player Rafael Nadal, who currently earns $14,000,000.

4

Tennis balls were originally all black or white but in 1972, the International Tennis Federation approved the change to yellow.

The main reason was that the game was beginning to become popular on TV but most broadcasts were still in black and white, which rendered the balls almost invisible.

Today's balls must not only be in a regulation colour, but weigh between 56 and 59.4 grams.

5

Unlike other sports, there aren't many variations on standard match rules.

This, coupled with passionate fans, makes for some pretty intense betting.

So much so that by 2021, online betting apps featured sections and themes dedicated to the sport, showing the popularity of tennis in the digital age.

6

Don Budge is considered one of the greatest tennis players of all time and the only man to win all four Grand Slam tournaments in the same year.

In addition to this, he is also the only male player in tennis history to have won six consecutive Grand Slam singles titles.

Budge's incredible achievement began in 1937, when he won the Wimbledon title, defeating Gottfried von Cramm in the final.

He then went on to win the US Open, the French Open, and the Australian Open in the same year, completing the Grand Slam.

Budge continued his winning streak in 1938, winning the Australian Open, the French Open, and Wimbledon, becoming the only male player in history to win six consecutive Grand Slam singles titles.

His streak finally came to an end when he lost in the final of the 1938 US Open to his compatriot, Bobby Riggs.

In addition to his Grand Slam successes, Budge also won numerous other major titles during his career, including the Davis Cup with the United States team on four occasions.

Overall, he won 10 Grand Slam singles titles in his career and is considered one of the greatest tennis players of all time.

Don Budge has left a lasting legacy on tennis, not just for his on-court achievements, but also for his innovative playing style and his focus on physical and mental preparation for the sport.

His ability to win six consecutive Grand Slam singles titles remains an incredible achievement and one that is difficult to match.

7

The 1877 Wimbledon Tennis Championships was a men's tennis tournament held at the All England Croquet and Lawn Tennis Club (AEC & LTC) in Wimbledon, London.

It was the world's first official lawn tennis tournament and was later recognised as the first Grand Slam or "Major" tournament.

The AEC & LTC was founded in July 1868, as the All England Croquet Club; lawn tennis was introduced in February 1875 to make up for the waning interest in croquet.

8

Women players are extremely competitive, both on and off the court.

One of the best remembered for winning the Golden Slam is Steffi Graf.

Until a few years ago the most famous of all was American Serena Williams, today she ranks eighth in the women's rankings, with Australia's Ashleigh Barty leading the way with an overwhelming score.

Barty's meteoric rise drove her earnings up from $2,823,371 in 2018 to $11,307,587 in 2019.

9

Roger Federer is considered one of the greatest tennis players of all time and one of the most complete players in the history of the sport.

In addition to his exceptional skills in the rest of the game, Federer also has one of the most precise and effective serves on the court, which has allowed him to score a large number of aces in his career.

To date, Federer has scored a total of 11,368 aces in his career, which places him third on the list of players with the most direct serves of all time.

However, he is still behind Croatian player Ivo Karlovic, who holds the first place with an impressive total of 13,687 aces in his career.

Federer has been very consistent in his ability to produce aces throughout his career, and his serve is considered one of the best on the professional circuit.

His ability to serve both from the baseline and from the net has allowed him to win many points quickly and efficiently.

Despite being in third place on the list of players with the most aces in history, Federer is still active on the circuit and has the opportunity to surpass Karlovic's record if he continues to play and produce aces throughout his career.

With his talent and dedication, it is possible that Federer will continue to add to his record of aces and remain one of the most dominant players in the sport of tennis.

10

Tennis elbow, also known as lateral epicondylitis, is a medical condition characterized by inflammation of the tendons that connect the muscles of the forearm to the outer part of the elbow.

This condition often occurs as a result of overuse or repetitive injury to the forearm muscles that cause tension and stress on the tendons.

Despite its name, tennis elbow not only affects tennis players.

In fact, the condition is very common in people who engage in activities that involve repetitive wrist and forearm movement, such as lifting heavy objects, doing manual labor, playing sports like golf, or even typing on a computer for extended periods of time.

Symptoms of tennis elbow may include pain on the outer part of the elbow, weakness in the arm, and difficulty gripping objects with the hand.

If left untreated, the condition can worsen and lead to significant limitation in the function of the affected arm and hand.

Treatment for tennis elbow may include rest, ice, physical therapy, anti-inflammatory medications, and occupational therapy.

In severe cases, surgery may be necessary.

With proper treatment and prevention, most people with tennis elbow can return to their normal activities without pain or restrictions.

11

Modern tennis is the sport played worldwide today and has its origins in Real Tennis, also known as "Jeu de Paume," which was played in Europe since the Middle Ages.

This game was played on an enclosed court with walls and a net in the middle, where players hit a ball with their hand or with a special racket.

Real Tennis was the most popular sport at the court of Henry VIII in the 16th century and became an elite activity in Europe for several centuries.

In the mid-19th century, a more modern version of the game was created, known as "lawn tennis," and was played outdoors on a grass surface.

This version was invented by the British Walter Clopton Wingfield and became a popular form of entertainment for the British upper class.

12

The word "tennis" has its origins in Old French and was derived from the word "tenez", which means "take" or "hold" in Spanish.

During the early days of tennis, players would pass the ball to each other, and to indicate that they were ready to start, they would say "tenez" before serving the ball.

Over time, the word became synonymous with the sport itself, and was used to refer to the activity rather than just indicating that the ball was being served.

As tennis spread throughout Europe and arrived in England, the word "tennis" was adopted in English and became the common term used for the sport.

The word "tennis" was first used in a book written by the Italian poet and humanist Francesco Berni in 1505.

Since then, the word "tennis" has been used worldwide to refer to the sport we know today.

13

Venus and Serena Williams are two of the most successful players in the history of women's tennis.

Both have won numerous Grand Slam titles and have been ranked as the world number one on several occasions.

At the Olympics, the two sisters have been very successful, especially in doubles.

In London 2012, Venus and Serena won the gold medal in women's doubles, making them the first tennis players to win four Olympic gold medals each.

Previously, the Williams sisters had also won the gold medal in women's doubles at Sydney 2000, Beijing 2008, and in London 2012.

With these four gold medals each, Venus and Serena Williams have broken the record for the most Olympic gold medals in tennis, both in the men's and women's draws.

In addition to their doubles success, Venus Williams also won the gold medal in singles at Sydney 2000, while Serena won the gold medal in singles at London 2012.

In total, the Williams sisters have won 9 combined Olympic gold medals.

14

Tennis rackets have evolved significantly over the years, from wooden rackets to modern carbon fiber or aluminum ones.

In the early days of tennis, rackets were much smaller and lighter, with a head size of around 65-70 square inches (approximately 419-452 square centimeters).

They were made of wood and had a simple frame structure.

Over time, rackets became larger and improved in terms of technology and materials.

In the 1970s, graphite rackets were introduced, which were lighter and more durable than wooden rackets.

Strings also evolved from sheep gut strings to synthetic materials, which offered more power and control.

Currently, tennis rackets are designed with advanced technologies and are made of materials like carbon fiber, ceramic, and tungsten.

There is also a wide variety of racket head sizes available, from smaller ones around 85 square inches (548 square centimeters) for advanced players, to larger ones around 115 square inches (741 square centimeters) for beginner players.

15

The Wimbledon Championships is one of the oldest and most prestigious tennis tournaments in the world.

It is played on the grass courts of the All England Lawn Tennis and Croquet Club in London, England, and is held annually in the month of July.

It was founded in 1877 and is one of the four Grand Slam tournaments, along with the Australian Open, the French Open (Roland Garros), and the US Open.

It is also worth noting that the Mexican Open Telcel is held in Acapulco, Mexico, and is one of the most important tournaments in Latin America.

It is played on hard courts and has been classified as an ATP 500 tournament, which means that players earn more points than in an ATP 250 tournament but fewer than in an ATP 1000 tournament.

The tournament has been played since 1993 and has featured the participation of notable players such as Rafael Nadal and Novak Djokovic.

16

The Grand Slam Cup was a trophy awarded to the player who managed to win all four Grand Slam tournaments in a single calendar year.

The term "Grand Slam" refers to winning the four major tennis tournaments worldwide: the Australian Open, Roland Garros, Wimbledon, and the US Open.

So far, only two players in the open era of tennis have managed to win all four Grand Slam tournaments in a single calendar year: Rod Laver in 1962 and 1969, and Steffi Graf in 1988.

Rafael Nadal is one of the greatest tennis players of all time and has won 20 Grand Slam titles in his career, tying with Roger Federer for the men's record.

Of the 20 titles, 13 have been won at Roland Garros, the clay tournament in France, making him the most successful player in the history of the tournament.

Nadal has also won four titles at the US Open, two at Wimbledon, and one at the Australian Open.

17

Many people wonder why tennis has a strange scoring system in games (15, 30, 40, game).

The answer lies in the sexagesimal system that uses the number 60 as the base arithmetic, with the need to win four points to win a game.

Initially, the score was counted as 15, 30, 45, and 60 (game).

Later, the 45 was replaced with 40 for its ease and speed of pronunciation.

18

Modern tennis was influenced by Real Tennis, also known as "court tennis" or "royal tennis," which originated in France in the 12th century.

However, the sport as we know it today was developed in England in the 19th century.

Modern tennis is believed to have originated in Warwickshire, in central England, in 1873, when Major Walter Clopton Wingfield patented the game and marketed it as "Sphairistike."

However, Captain Harry Gem and Spanish player Augurio Perea, both Real Tennis players, also played an important role in the evolution of modern tennis.

In 1865, they created a simplified version of Real Tennis that could be played outdoors on a grass court, and called it "lawn tennis."

They also established the basic rules of the game, including the use of a net and a rubber ball.

From then on, the game quickly became popular in England and around the world, and became an Olympic sport at the Athens Games in 1896.

Since then, tennis has evolved significantly, from wooden rackets and rubber balls to modern carbon fiber rackets and high-tech balls.

19

The evolution of tennis rackets has been significant in the history of this sport.

Although wooden rackets were the most common during much of the 20th century, the introduction of synthetic and composite materials in racket manufacturing has allowed for greater power and control in shots.

The first wooden tennis rackets were small and heavy, and the strings were made of animal gut.

As players began to require more power and speed in their shots, larger and lighter rackets with synthetic strings were developed.

By the early 1980s, most professional players had already made the transition to graphite and composite rackets.

Yannick Noah's wooden racket, which won the French Open in 1983, is considered the last great achievement of a wooden racket in elite tennis.

Today, most tennis players use carbon fiber and composite rackets that are lighter and more durable than wooden rackets.

20

The shortest tennis match in history was played in 1988 at the Roland Garros tournament, where Frenchman Christian Boussus defeated German Bernard Mignot 6-0, 6-0, 6-0 in just 18 minutes.

As for the longest match, it was in the first round of the Wimbledon tournament in 2010, where American John Isner and Frenchman Nicolas Mahut played an epic match that lasted 11 hours and 5 minutes, extending over three days due to the lack of natural light and being suspended several times due to bad weather.

The fifth set of the match lasted over 8 hours, and Isner finally won 70-68 in the fifth set.

This match is considered one of the most memorable events in the history of tennis.

21

Pete Sampras, born in the United States in 1971, is considered one of the greatest tennis players of all time.

During his career, he won 14 Grand Slam titles, including seven at Wimbledon, and held the world number one ranking for a total of 286 weeks, making him the player with the most time in that position in the history of tennis.

Sampras began his professional career in 1988 and won his first Grand Slam title at the 1990 US Open.

Throughout his career, he also won five titles at the US Open, two at the Australian Open, and one title at the Roland Garros.

His rivalry with player Andre Agassi was one of the most famous in the history of tennis, and their Grand Slam final matchups were highly anticipated by fans of the sport.

Although Pete Sampras retired in 2002, his record of weeks as world number one was surpassed in 2004 by Swiss player Roger Federer, who has held that position for a total of 310 weeks.

However, Sampras is still considered one of the greatest tennis players of all time, and his legacy in the sport continues to be remembered and admired by fans around the world.

22

To find the oldest tennis player, we have to go to Mexico and meet José Guadalupe Leal Lemus, who has been playing regularly at Club Campestre Morelia for 79 of his 101 years.

Nowadays, he only plays on Wednesdays with a group of younger doctors.

As for the professional circuit, although not a player, Manny Hershkowitz stands out as an American who worked as a ball boy at the age of 82.

23

John McEnroe and Stefan Edberg are the only players to have achieved number one rankings in both singles and doubles.

In recent years, professional tennis has become so specialized that playing doubles seems like a completely different sport, even though it is played on the same courts as singles tournaments.

It is very rare to see the world's top singles players competing in doubles matches and vice versa.

Michael Llodra, Radek Stepanek, Jurgen Melzer, and now Marcel Granollers frequently combine the individual and doubles circuits and have a prominent place in both rankings.

24

An ace is a serve that sends the ball into the opponent's court without being touched.

The record for the most aces in a single match was set by American player John Isner during his match against Nicolas Mahut in the first round of Wimbledon in 2010.

Isner achieved a total of 113 aces, while Mahut got 103, adding up to an astonishing total of 216 aces in the match.

This match is also known as the longest in tennis history, lasting for 11 hours and 5 minutes and played over three days.

25

Bill Tilden is considered one of the greatest tennis players in history, and it is rumored that he hit the fastest serve in tennis history in 1931, with a speed of 163.4 mph (263 km/h).

However, as you mentioned, the measuring tool used at that time was questionable, so it cannot be confirmed if that was the actual value reached.

On the other hand, in 2011, Croatian player Ivo Karlovic hit a verified serve at a speed of 156 mph (251 km/h) in a Davis Cup match against Germany, becoming the player who holds the record for the fastest serve in tennis history.

26

The 2012 Australian Open final between Rafael Nadal and Novak Djokovic was an epic battle that lasted 5 hours and 53 minutes, becoming the longest Grand Slam match in history.

Djokovic won 5-7, 6-4, 6-2, 6-7 (5), 7-5 in a match that was interrupted by rain for over an hour.

This match is also famous for its spectacular gameplay, as both players gave it their all, running all over the court and demonstrating their skills on every point.

The 2012 Australian Open final remains one of the most exciting matches in tennis history.

27

The world record for time in the air hitting a tennis ball is an event in which two or more players pass the tennis ball back and forth without it touching the ground or going out of bounds.

Ettore Rossetti and Angelo A. Rossetti decided to set the world record in 1978 in Connecticut, United States.

For 15 hours, the two men passed the ball without it touching the ground, achieving a total of 25,944 hits.

This event is known as the "flying tennis ball marathon" and is an impressive feat of skill, physical and mental endurance.

The record has been surpassed several times since then, but the Rossetti brothers' achievement remains impressive.

28

The US Open is one of the four most important tennis tournaments, known as Grand Slams, along with the Australian Open, French Open, and Wimbledon.

It is the last Grand Slam of the season and takes place in late August and early September.

The first edition of the tournament was played at the Newport Casino in Rhode Island in 1881 on grass courts and was called the US National Championship.

In 1915, the tournament moved to its current location in Flushing Meadows, Queens, New York.

The grass courts were replaced with clay courts and then with fast hard courts in 1978.

The main court of the US Open is Arthur Ashe Stadium, named after the African American tennis player who won the tournament in 1968, becoming the first black player to win a Grand Slam.

The stadium has a capacity of over 23,000 spectators and is the largest tennis stadium in the world.

Another important court at the US Open is Louis Armstrong Stadium, named after the famous jazz musician.

The stadium has a capacity of over 14,000 spectators and has been the site of some of the most exciting matches in tennis history.

29

Since 1973, the winners of the men's and women's categories at the US Open have received equal prize money.

This made the New York tournament the first Grand Slam to equalize the prize for both genders.

The winners of the men's and women's tournaments receive $3.7 million, while the runner-up earns $1.8 million.

Currently, all Grand Slams pay equally to all participants in the singles and doubles draws.

However, this policy of equal prize money was not implemented simultaneously.

The US Open introduced it in 1973, 34 years before Wimbledon did.

The Australian Open and French Open took 39 years to implement it.

30

Manuel "Manolo" Santana was born in Madrid, Spain, in 1938.

He started playing tennis at the age of 11 and quickly stood out as one of the best Spanish tennis players of his generation.

In 1961, he won his first major title, the Italian Open, and a year later he won his first Grand Slam at the Roland Garros tournament in Paris.

In 1965, Manolo Santana became the first Spaniard to win the US Open, defeating South African Cliff Drysdale in the final 6-2, 7-9, 7-5, 6-1.

With this victory, Santana completed his collection of Grand Slam titles, which included Roland Garros (1961 and 1964) and Wimbledon (1966).

Santana was also a key member of the Spanish Davis Cup team in the 1960s, helping Spain win the trophy in 1965 and 1967.

In total, Santana won 54 individual titles and 16 doubles titles in his professional career.

After retiring from tennis in 1973, Santana dedicated himself to coaching other players, including Sergi Bruguera, Arantxa Sánchez Vicario, and Juan Carlos Ferrero.

He also became an entrepreneur and founded the Manolo Santana Tennis Club in Marbella, Spain, where an annual ATP tournament is held.

In 1985, he was inducted into the International Tennis Hall of Fame.

31

The US Open has pioneered many innovations in tennis.

In 1975, it became the first Grand Slam to introduce night matches, allowing fans to enjoy more tennis and players to avoid the high temperatures of New York summer.

Additionally, the US Open is the only Grand Slam tournament that uses a tiebreak in the fifth set to break a tie, making matches more exciting and avoiding players having to play endless service games in a deciding set.

Regarding technology, the US Open was the first Grand Slam tournament to adopt Hawk-Eye technology on all of its courts, allowing players to challenge line calls in case of doubt.

It was also the first Grand Slam to implement the 25-second shot clock for players between serves, with the aim of speeding up the pace of matches and avoiding long pauses between points.

Moreover, the tournament's main stadium, the Arthur Ashe Stadium, is the largest tennis stadium in the world, with a capacity of over 23,000 spectators.

The US Open is held at the Billie Jean King National Tennis Center in Flushing Meadows, Queens, New York.

32

Arantxa Sánchez Vicario is one of the most prominent Spanish tennis players in history.

She was born in Barcelona in 1971 and began playing tennis at a very young age, just 4 years old.

At the age of 16, in 1987, she became a professional and since then started accumulating successes on the circuit.

In 1994, Arantxa Sánchez Vicario made history by winning the US Open in the women's singles category.

In the final, she faced German player Steffi Graf, one of the best tennis players of the time, and managed to defeat her in three very competitive sets, with a final score of 1-6, 7-6(3) and 6-4.

With this triumph, she became the first Spanish woman to win the New York tournament.

In addition to the US Open, Arantxa Sánchez Vicario won three other Grand Slam tournaments in singles: Roland Garros in 1989, 1994, and 1998, and the Australian Open in 1994.

She also won the mixed doubles title at Wimbledon in 1991, and the gold medal at the Barcelona 1992 Olympics in the doubles category with Conchita Martínez.

In her career, Arantxa Sánchez Vicario won a total of 29 singles titles and 69 doubles titles, reaching the world number 1 ranking in the WTA on several occasions.

She is considered one of the best Spanish tennis players of all time and one of the most important in the history of women's tennis.

33

Getting a US Open ball is a very valuable memory for tennis fans.

The tournament has an "open ball" policy, which means that balls are changed after a certain number of games and used balls are distributed for sale or given to spectators as souvenirs.

The tournament also has an official store where you can buy official US Open balls, as well as other souvenirs such as t-shirts, hats, souvenirs, etc.

Additionally, during the tournament, autograph sessions and player meet and greets are also organized, where you can get signatures and photos as a memory.

34

Rafael Nadal is considered one of the most successful tennis players in the history of the sport, and his record at the US Open backs it up.

In 2010, he won his first title at the US Open after defeating Serbian Novak Djokovic in the final in four sets.

In 2013, he defeated Djokovic again in the final in four sets.

In 2017, he defeated Kevin Anderson in the final in three sets to achieve his third title in New York.

In 2019, Nadal won his fourth title at the US Open after an exciting final in which he overcame Russian Daniil Medvedev in five sets.

In addition, Nadal has been a finalist on three other occasions at the US Open, in 2011, 2018, and 2021, and has been a semifinalist four more times.

With his four titles, Nadal is the second Spanish player to win the US Open after Manolo Santana, and one of the few tennis players in history to win all four Grand Slam tournaments.

35

Neither the First nor the Second World War, nor the coronavirus epidemic were able to stop the biggest tournament in the United States.

The US Open has been held for 140 years, making it the only Grand Slam that has never been suspended.

The rest of the majors have had their schedules altered by war and by the pandemic that has been sweeping the world since 2019.

36

The United States Tennis Association announced an increase in prize money for the Grand Slam.

The event offers $57.5 million in prizes for players.

In addition, nearly $6 million is distributed during the qualifying rounds, which is beneficial for players who do not advance too far in the early stages of the tournament.

This will mean an increase of 65.7% compared to the previous edition.

37

Wimbledon is the only one of the four Grand Slams not organised by a national federation, as are Australia, Roland Garros and the US Open, but by a club.

The All England Lawn Tennis Club, originally founded on 23 July 1868 as a croquet club.

Croquet involves hitting wooden or plastic balls with a mallet through metal hoops planted around the playing field The club has a maximum of 500 full, life and honorary members.

38

Until 2019, a Wimbledon committee reserved the right to choose the seeded players in both singles and doubles based on their previous performances in the grass-court campaign, and not solely on their position in the world rankings.

This is the same as the selection process for the other Grand Slams, and is the second year that they have been chosen this way.

The old system meant that, for example, Roger Federer was ranked higher than Rafa Nadal in the draw, even though the Spaniard was above the Swiss in the rankings.

39

One of the most legendary and controversial aspects of Wimbledon is the Dress Code, the dress code that requires all players to wear outfits in which the predominant color is white, including sneakers and all accessories such as headbands, wristbands, caps...

Only small bands of other colors, up to a maximum of 10 millimeters, are allowed.

Members and guests of the tournament are required to attend in a jacket, tie, and respectable-looking trousers.

40

Wimbledon ballboys and ballgirls, known as BBGs, are 250 volunteers from different British schools and institutions, including the charitable organization DR. Barnardos, which takes in boys and girls in vulnerable situations.

The balls are supplied by the firm Slazinger since 1902.

It is the longest-lasting sponsorship link in sports history and approximately 55,000 balls are made for thetournament each year.

41

Roger Federer holds nine titles and Martina Navratilova holds eight, making them the greatest champions in Wimbledon history.

The youngest champion was Boris Becker in 1985 at the age of 17 years and 22 days.

The youngest ladies champion was Lottie Dod, who won in 1888 at the age of 15 years and 285 days.

In terms of consecutive trophies, the leaders are still William Renshaw and Navratilova with six.

42

Spain has won five Wimbledon titles so far: Rafa Nadal (2008 and 2010), Manolo Santana (1966), Conchita Martínez (1994) and Garbiñe Muguruza (2017).

Nadal has reached the finals three times (2006, 2007 and 2011), Lili Álvarez three times (1926, 1927 and 1928), Arantxa Sánchez Vicario twice (1995 and 1996), and Muguruza once (2015).

Arantxa Sánchez Vicario also won the doubles title, along with Czech Jana Novotna, in 1995.

43

During the tennis match between Tommy Haas and Jiri Vesely at the 2017 Miami Open, an iguana appeared on the court and caused an interruption in the game.

The iguana, which was approximately one meter in length, walked around the court before stopping on one of the court's walls.

The tournament workers tried to remove it, but the iguana seemed unwilling to move.

It was then when Tommy Haas, who was on the court at that time, decided to take advantage of the situation and take a selfie with the reptile, which he posted on his Instagram account.

Finally, the iguana was removed from the court, and the match could continue.

The incident became viral on social media and a memorable moment of that tournament.

44

Serbian Novak Djokovic closed the match against Joao Sousa without any problem, on a day marked by rain that forced the match to be suspended for an hour and a half.

However, the most remarkable thing about the match was not the suspension for so long.

The world number 2 allowed himself to joke with one of the ball boys during one of the breaks in the match, to the delight of the Philippe Chatrier crowd.

Djokovic surprised the entire audience by inviting a ball boy to sit next to him.

The young boy accepted the invitation, but not without first putting on a surprised face, and they exchanged objects.

Novak took the umbrella that the ball boy was holding and the boy took Djokovic's racket.

The Serbian spent a few minutes chatting and having a drink with the young boy, even asking if he wanted anything to drink, earning applause from the fans.

45

In an exhibition doubles match involving Kim Clijsters and Conchita Martínez, a spectator in the audience kept criticizing the serves.

Then, the Spanish tennis player and the Belgian offered him a racket and invited him to come down to the court and demonstrate his skills.

Since the rules of Wimbledon require players to wear white, Clijsters offered the man... one of her skirts, resulting in a very funny image, which the commentator described as: "A man in a skirt trying to defend a serve from Kim Clijsters.

Friends, this is 2017." Clijsters, a former professional tennis player, elite player between 1999 and 2012, and winner of three Grand Slams in singles and two in doubles, Wimbledon and Roland Garros made three serves.

The spectator, with great difficulty, managed to return one in a poor manner.

46

In 2012, the Plaza de Toros at Roland Garros, one of the most iconic courts of the complex that hosts the Paris Grand Slam, debuted an unusual appearance by dyeing the traditional red clay a bubblegum pink.

This was done to honor female athletes on International Women's Day in France.

In addition to changing the usual playing surface, the tournament invited several of the most famous former female tennis players to play matches on this court.

The godmother of the event was Chris Evert, winner of the prestigious French tournament seven times.

47

In 2005, the USTA decided to change the color of the tennis courts at the US Open from green to blue, seeking better visibility for players and spectators, as well as a distinction from other American tournaments.

The change was made with an acrylic surface called "DecoTurf," which is also used in other major tournaments such as the Australian Open.

Additionally, in 2019, the USTA announced that they would return to green on the Arthur Ashe Stadium center court to celebrate the 50th anniversary of the stadium.

However, the surface remains the same "DecoTurf."

48

The US Open has been played on three different surfaces since it began in 1881.

From then until 1974 the tournament was played on grass, but with the move to the West Side Tennis Club in Forest Hills, the fourth Grand Slam of each year was played on clay.

In 1978, Flushing Meadows took over the tournament, changing the surface yet again to a hard court.

49

Right-handed tennis players have won a total of 102 titles at the US Open, while left-handers have done so in only 24.

It is interesting to note that although right-handed tennis players have won many more titles at the US Open than left-handers, some of the most successful players in the history of this tournament are left-handed, such as Rafael Nadal and Jimmy Connors, both with 4 titles in their careers.

Overall, it is believed that left-handed players have a certain advantage in tennis because their playing style is less common and may be more difficult for right-handed players to adapt to.

50

The streak of right-handers dominating the US Open for 22 years began in 1985 when Ivan Lendl won his first title in New York and ended in 2006 with the victory of Swiss player Roger Federer.

During this period, right-handers won a total of 11 titles in 22 consecutive years.

In contrast, left-handers have won a total of 24 US Open titles.

Of these, four left-handed players have dominated on 11 occasions: Jimmy Connors won 5 titles, John McEnroe won 4, Rafael Nadal has won 3, and Guillermo Vilas won the title once.

51

The record of seven titles at the US Open, achieved by right-handers, is shared by three American tennis players: Richard D. Sears, William A. Larned, and William T. Tilden.

Sears was the first champion in the tournament's history, winning seven consecutive editions between 1881 and 1887.

Larned won two titles in 1901 and 1902 and then another five between 1907 and 1911.

Tilden, on the other hand, won six titles between 1920 and 1925, and then another one in 1929.

All of them are members of the International Tennis Hall of Fame.

52

The most successful left-hander is American Jimmy Connors, who has five wins to his name: 1974, 1976, 1978, 1982 and 1983.

Only 10% of the world's population is left-handed.

However, since the beginning of the so-called "Open Era", left-handed tennis players have won twenty-two of the ninety-six singles titles at the prestigious Wimbledon tournament: 23%.

53

Right-handed women have won 113 titles while only seven have gone to left-handers.

The most successful right-handed player was Norwegian Molla B. Mallory, 1915-18, 1920-22, 1926, with eight.

The most successful left-hander was American Martina Navratilova, with four (1983-83, 1986-87).

54

The dominance of right-handed players lasted for 75 years from 1908-1982, during which twenty-four women won while left-handed players only established their dominance for two-year periods:

in 1983-84 and 1986-87 by American Martina Navratilova and 1991-92 by her Croatian-born compatriot Monica Seles.

55

Norwegian Molla B. Mallory was a standout tennis player of the 1920s who won a total of eight US Open titles, becoming the right-handed female player with the most victories in the tournament's history.

On the other hand, the most successful left-handed female player in the tournament's history is American Martina Navratilova, who won a total of four US Open titles in the 1983, 1984, 1986, and 1987 editions.

Navratilova is considered one of the greatest tennis players of all time and is remembered for her talent, charisma, and dominance of the game in the 1980s.

56

Venus Williams holds the record for the fastest female serve in a Grand Slam tournament.

Williams' fastest serve was recorded at the 2008 Wimbledon Championships, where she reached a speed of 205 kilometers per hour.

Additionally, the overall fastest serve record in women's tennis belongs to German player Sabine Lisicki, who registered a serve of 211 kilometers per hour at the 2014 Bank of the West Classic tournament in Stanford.

57

Henry Wilfred "Bunny" Austin (26 August 1906 - 26 August 2000) was an English player.

For seventy-four years he was the last Briton to reach the men's singles final at Wimbledon , until Andy Murray did so in 2012.

He was also a finalist at the 1937 French Open Championships and a winner of the championship in Queen's Club.

Along with Fred Perry, he was a vital part of the British team that won the Davis Cup in three consecutive years (1933-1935) and is also remembered as the first player to wear shorts at Wimbledon in 1932.

58

Wimbledon is one of the oldest and most prestigious tennis tournaments in the world, and is considered by many to be the most important of the four Grand Slam events.

It is held annually at the All England Lawn Tennis and Croquet Club in the Wimbledon neighborhood of South London, England.

Wimbledon is the only Grand Slam tournament played on grass courts, which gives it a unique and special character.

The grass, which is cut to a height of 8 mm, gives the ball a low and fast bounce, making matches exciting and very fast-paced.

The tournament is played in five categories: men's and women's singles, men's and women's doubles, and mixed doubles.

Singles matches are played best of five sets, while doubles matches are best of three sets.

59

Margaret Smith Court is considered one of the greatest tennis players of all time and one of the greatest champions of all time.

Born in Australia in 1942, she began her professional career in 1960 and retired in 1977.

During her career, she won a total of 64 Grand Slam titles in singles, doubles, and mixed doubles.

Court won 24 Grand Slam singles titles, the most for any player in the history of tennis.

Among her titles are 11 French Open titles, 5 Australian Open titles, 3 Wimbledon titles, and 5 US Open titles.

In addition, Court won 19 Grand Slam doubles titles and 21 Grand Slam mixed doubles titles, bringing her total to 64.

She is also the only player in history to have won a Calendar Year Golden Slam in mixed doubles, meaning she won all four Grand Slam titles and the Olympic gold medal in the same season in 1965.

After retiring from tennis, Court became a Christian pastor and has been criticized for her homophobic comments.

Due to her comments, there have been calls to change the name of the main court at the Australian Open, which currently bears her name.

60

Wimbledon and fashion have had a complicated relationship over the years.

With no rules in its origins, ladies wore hats and long dresses closed up to the neck, while starched shirts and long pants were the most chosen attire for gentlemen, although Harold Mahoney appeared in 1896 with socks of different colors.

In 1887, Lottie Dod was the first woman to benefit from a more sporty outfit.

At just 15 years old and being in school, Lottie was allowed to play with a shorter dress and without a hat, with just a simple cap.

She won her first Wimbledon against Blanche Bingley, a lady who was said to never touch fish with a knife or the ball with bare hands, so she played with percale gloves.

61

Arthur Ashe was one of the great American tennis players of the 1960s and 1970s, winner of three Grand Slam tournaments: the Australian Open (1970), Wimbledon (1975), and the US Open (1968).

In the 1968 edition of the US Open, Ashe became the first African-American tennis player to win a Grand Slam tournament in the Open Era.

In addition to his achievements on the court, Ashe was known for his social and political activism.

He was an advocate for civil rights and racial equality, and also advocated for education and access to sports for low-income youth and marginalized communities.

In 1992, Ashe was inducted into the International Tennis Hall of Fame in recognition of his athletic achievements and social activism.

Sadly, Ashe passed away in 1993 at the age of 49 due to complications related to HIV, which he contracted after receiving a blood transfusion during heart surgery in 1983.

62

The function of plastic grommets is to protect the strings from rubbing against the frame of the racket.

If the grommet deteriorates, the strings could suffer premature breakage.

This string-racket friction can also create looseness in the holes and render the racket unusable.

Depending on the type of racket we have, the grommets will be wider or narrower; if it is a power racket, we will have wider grommets, as the strings will need greater freedom of movement.

If it is a control racket, the strings will need to move less and, therefore, will require narrower grommets.

63

One of Rafa Nadal's strange routines is to adjust his pants before serving, touch one of his shoulders, sometimes both, fix his hair behind his ears, touch his nose, and bounce the ball.

He sweeps the baseline with his foot a little bit, in case of playing on clay.

Another well-known ritual is to meticulously arrange two bottles, one next to the other, standing in front of his bench.

64

Russian tennis player Maria Sharapova, between points, does not step on the lines, adjusts her strings with her back to the court, takes a turn and does a few small jumps before playing the point.

Additionally, before serving, she always makes sure to adjust her hair and bounce the ball gently.

She is also famous for always carrying a towel with her onto the court and wiping off sweat during every break between games or sets.

Sharapova has stated that these rituals help her concentrate and feel comfortable on the court.

She has also mentioned that some of them, like adjusting her racket strings, give her a sense of control and security before each point.

65

Serena Williams, one of the most successful tennis players in history, is known for being very detail-oriented and having certain obsessions before and during matches.

One of her peculiarities is that she often wears the same socks throughout an entire tournament, which has been a source of surprise and amusement among her colleagues on the circuit.

Additionally, she always carries a pair of shower sandals in her tennis bag to use after matches and avoid walking barefoot in public areas.

Williams is also known for her strict routine before each match, which includes a detailed and specific warm-up, a five-minute ritual for tying her shoes, and a series of specific movements and gestures that she performs before each serve.

Additionally, Williams is very superstitious and believes that certain elements and objects bring her luck, such as a tennis ball she carries in her bag that has special meaning to her.

Her obsession is such that, at times, she attributes her loss to not following her routine.

66

Novak Djokovic used to imitate his colleagues on the court from time to time, but he has stopped doing so.

"There came a time when I said I had to stop clowning around and focus on playing tennis. Maybe I'll do it if the timing is right during training, but I have to be careful not to offend anyone. The goal was simply to laugh and joke around."

67

John Isner bounces the ball between his legs just before serving.

"One habit that I've always had is the one where I bounce the ball between my legs before serving. It's not something I think about, it's not a conscious movement. I just know that doing it helps me get into a rhythm, especially with my serve."

68

Roger Federer, considered one of the greatest tennis players of all time and the male player with the most Grand Slam titles in tennis history, is known for his rituals and superstitions before and during matches.

In addition to carrying eight rackets in his tennis bag, Federer has several rituals that he performs before each match, including hitting a specific number of aces during warm-up.

Another one of his rituals includes always putting on the same leg of his pants and the same sleeve of his shirt first, and he also changes rackets after every service game.

Additionally, Federer always wipes sweat from his face with a towel before every serve, and in Grand Slam tournaments, he always wears a long-sleeved shirt during warm-up, even on the hottest days.

69

One player well known for his quirks was Björn Borg.

"I didn't shave during tournaments. During matches I would feel my headband between points, pinch the strings and bang my racket against my shoes. These were little rituals that helped me to let my mind go blank and just focus on the game," the Swede said.

From 1976 to 1980, at every Wimbledon he played in, he grew a beard and wore the same Fila-branded shirt; he won them all in those five years, setting the record which he shares with Federer, for the highest number of consecutive Wimbledon wins in the Open era.

70

On "The Clare Balding Show," Ilie Nastase recalled an anecdote from his career:

"I knew that Italians were very superstitious about black cats. A few weeks ago, we were in Monte Carlo on our way to a restaurant. On the way there, in a line of three cars, the one in front stopped, which was Italian, and explained that in Italy when a black cat appears in front of the car, you have to turn around. When Roland Garros began, we faced Adriano Panatta and Paolo Bertolucci, two Italians, in the first round. Then I told Mabrouk, the locker room attendant, that I would pay him 500 francs if he could get a black cat. First, he brought a gray one, but after paying him another 500, he got a black one. When we went out onto the court, the cat was in my bag. Then, before the match started, I told the umpire that I had a problem with my racket, then I went, opened my bag, the cat came out and ran straight towards Pannata, who couldn't get any balls into the court."

Nastase won that match, with his partner Bob Hewitt, 6-2 and 6-4.

71

Tennis player James Blake went through a tough time when he broke his neck during training in Rome.

When he was in the hospital, the tournament doctor came to visit him and brought a very special note from Roger Federer.

"I hope you're feeling better, sorry to hear what happened."

This emotional gesture meant a lot to Blake, and when he could, he went to thank Federer and told him, "It means a lot to me that you really care about your colleagues."

72

Andre Agassi had a goal imposed by his father, who dreamed of turning him into the number 1 in the world.

When Andre was seven years old, he had to hit 2,500 balls a day.

According to Agassi's father's calculations, this would amount to a million hits a year, which meant, in the patriarch's mind:

"A child who can hit 1 million balls a year will be unbeatable."

73

Agassi joined the Bollettieri Academy, where some of the biggest sports promises trained.

During his stay at the academy, he rebelled against the imposed rules.

Once, at a tournament in Florida, he entered the court wearing jeans, earrings, and eyeliner.

Regardless of this, he defeated his opponent.

74

Agassi managed to break the rules of the Bollettieri Academy a bit, thanks to a stuffed panda bear he won during his visit to Busch Gardens, inside Disney in Tampa, Florida.

The gym owner, Nick, wanted to buy the stuffed animal from Agassi for his daughter, but André did not sell it.

He made a trade: he gave the bear in exchange for Nick's daughter studying remotely and receiving invitations to play tournaments abroad.

75

Agassi turned professional in 1986, winning his first title almost a year later, with Brazil being the country where he won his first championship.

The American entered the ATP of Itaparica, in Bahia, as a guest and advanced to the final to face Brazilian Luiz Mattar.

In two sets with a score of 7-6 and 6-2, he won the $90,000 prize, starting the story of his victories.

In his career, Agassi won 60 titles.

76

The rivalry between Andre Agassi and Pete Sampras is considered one of the greatest in the history of men's tennis.

The two players faced each other a total of 34 times, with Sampras winning 20 of them and Agassi 14.

Sampras and Agassi were two very different players in style and personality.

Sampras was a more traditional player, with a great serve and effective volley game, while Agassi was known for his baseline play and ability to return difficult shots.

Among the most memorable matches between Sampras and Agassi is the 2002 US Open final, in which Sampras won in four sets to claim his 15th and final Grand Slam title.

The quarterfinal match at Wimbledon in 1993, which lasted over five hours and was won by Sampras in five sets, is also remembered.

Despite their on-court rivalry, Sampras and Agassi have spoken well of each other off the court, and have collaborated on several charitable projects together.

77

Agassi went from having long hair at the beginning of his career to being completely bald during his last years as a professional.

The tennis player used a wig to disguise his baldness and maintain his unique style.

In 1994, convinced by his then-girlfriend and later wife, Brooke Shields, he stopped using the wig and had a ceremony at his home to shave his head.

A year later, he began playing with a shaved head.

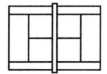

78

Although Sampras was Agassi's biggest rival, it was with Boris Becker that things went further.

The hatred was such that in 1995, after reading his enemy's statements in the newspapers, Agassi spent the entire summer training to fulfill his main purpose: to eliminate Becker from the US Open in New York.

Achieving his goal, the "Summer of Revenge" ended with André eliminating the German in the semifinals of the tournament.

However, Sampras won the title.

79

In his autobiography, Agassi admits to having always been in love with Steffi Graf, the German who won twenty-two Grand Slams and is one of the best players in the history of tennis.

His first chance to get close to her was in 1992, when they both won at Wimbledon.

Back then, tradition was that the men's and women's champions danced together at the formal tournament party held at the All England Club.

Agassi won the first major title of his career and prepared to finally meet his muse and accompany her on the dance floor, but his luck ran out when the dance was cancelled.

Fate brought the two together in 1999, when they broke with their partners and began the story that continues today.

They have been married since 2001 and have two children.

80

Before his relationship with Steffi Graf, Agassi was married for two years to Brooke Shields but their marriage ended so badly that he was convinced by a so-called friend to try methamphetamine.

Agassi had to write a letter explaining his use of drugs to avoid a three-month suspension.

The letter didn't tell the real story though. Agassi said he'd accidentally drunk a soda and thought the drugs would flush through his system quickly.

The ATP considered the letter carefully and decided to acquit him without any punishment.

81

It happened at the Atlantic Tire Championships and the protagonist of the curious incident was Tennys Sandgren.

Only 15 minutes of the match had been played when Sandgren, one of the caddies, returned a ball that had hit him in the groin.

The American's reaction was to hit the ball with his racket, inadvertently hitting one of the judges.

The Argentine newspaper "La Nación" pointed out that "immediately Sandgren threw the racket, apologized, and walked to the position of umpire Roger Pennington. After confirming that the ball had hit one of the officials, although no images were recorded, it was decided to expel him from the tournament."

The tennis player, beyond what happened, commented on the particular episode on his Twitter account.

He wrote: "Well, tonight I was hit in the balls by a mustard-covered ball. I threw it against the fence and it hit a referee as he walked to the other side, which resulted in a penalty. How's your night going?"

82

It is said that in 1999, during the Roland Garros tournament, Andre Agassi forgot to pack his underwear and had no choice but to play without it.

Despite the initial discomfort, he won the match and decided to continue playing without underwear from that moment on, as he felt more comfortable without it.

This decision became one of his superstitions and throughout the rest of his career, he was seen playing without underwear.

83

Nick Bollettieri is one of the most prominent coaches in the history of tennis.

He was born in 1931 in Pelham, New York, and began his tennis career as a player at the University of Miami.

Later, in the 1970s, he founded the famous Bollettieri Academy in Bradenton, Florida, which became an elite training center for young tennis players around the world.

Bollettieri has coached some of the best players in the history of tennis, including Andre Agassi, Jim Courier, Monica Seles, Mary Pierce, Boris Becker, Martina Hingis, and Serena Williams, among others.

He has also coached the US Davis Cup team and worked as a television commentator.

Bollettieri has been praised for his aggressive and demanding coaching style, and criticized by some for his focus on teaching a very physical and power-focused style of play, to the detriment of technique and tactical play.

Despite the criticisms, it cannot be denied that he has had a great impact on the world of tennis, and many of his students have gone on to become Grand Slam champions and sports stars.

84

It was first played in 1905 under the name Australian Championships.

With the "Open Era", its name was changed to Australian Open.

Roy Emerson, with 5 consecutive titles in 1963-1967, and Margaret Court, with 7 consecutive titles in 1960-1966, hold the records for consecutive victories.

The women's trophy is named "Daphne Akhurst Memorial Cup" in honor of the Sydney player who won 5 titles.

The men's trophy, "Norman Brookes Challenge Cup", is named after the first Australian player to excel outside Oceania.

Its venue has moved to six different locations between Australia (Perth, Brisbane, Adelaide, Sydney and Melbourne) and New Zealand (Christchurch and Hastings).

Melbourne Park has two main courts, the Rod Laver Arena, Australian player of the 60s and 70s, and the Hisense Arena.

85

Tennis players who love bright colours or exuberant outfits are not allowed to wear them at Wimbledon.

The tournament has a dress code which demands all players must wear white.

1877 was the first championship held and was won by Spencer Gore.

Twenty two tennis players took part in front of two hundred spectators.

Wimbledon is the oldest of the four Grand Slams.

A famous fact of the tournament is the quintessential dessert of strawberries and cream.

It is said that King George V introduced the dessert and it has remained a Grand Slam staple, with approximately twenty-four tonnes of strawberries consumed every year.

Switzerland's Roger Federer, with eight titles, and Martina Navratilova of the United States, with nine, are the most-crowned tennis players at the tournament.

Another Wimbledon tradition is that since 1902, the only official ball has been the Slazenger ball, making the brand the oldest sponsorship linked to the sport.

86

The French Open is the only Grand Slam played on clay, and Spanish tennis player Rafael Nadal is lord and master of the surface, with twelve Roland Garros titles.

The name has nothing to do with tennis, but was named after Roland Garros, a French aviator and war hero who died in combat during the First World War.

The last French tennis player to win Roland Garros was Yannick Noa in 1983.

The winner's trophy and one of the main courts at Roland Garros are named after French tennis great Suzanne Lenglen, who dominated the sport between 1919 and 1926.

The Roland Garros champion takes home the Musketeers' Cup, named after the four French tennis players René Lacoste, Henri Cochet, Jean Borotra and Jacques Brugnon, who won the Davis Cup in 1927.

87

The winner of the first seven trophies in the United States was Richard Sears, all of them consecutively, a feat no one else has ever managed to repeat.

Now known as the Billie Jean King National Tennis Center since 2006 and located in Flushing Meadows, it has hosted the US Open for the past forty-two years.

It is the only Grand Slam to have been played on all three surfaces.

From 1881 to 1974, the tournament was held on grass, then from 1975 to 1977 it was played on clay, and with the change of venue it is still played on hard court today.

It was the first Grand Slam to pay the same for the winners of the men's and women's championships in 1973.

It was also the first Grand Slam with hawk eye on all courts, and in 2018 the technology was introduced to every court in case there are doubts about the judge's decision.

88

Roberto Bautista Agut is a Spanish professional tennis player born on April 14, 1988 in Castellón de la Plana.

From a very young age, he dedicated himself to tennis and quickly stood out on the junior circuit, becoming world number 4 in 2006.

In the professional circuit, Bautista Agut has won several titles in singles and doubles, and reached his best position in the world ranking at number 9 in July 2019.

One of his greatest achievements has been defeating Novak Djokovic on several occasions, which is considered a great milestone given the Serbian's level of play and his position as world number 1.

Bautista Agut is known for his tenacity and ability to defend every ball with great energy and determination, which makes him a very difficult opponent to beat.

Additionally, he is a very complete player who dominates both the game from the baseline and the game at the net.

His career has been consistent and it is expected that he will continue to surprise and achieve success in the future.

89

The Davis Cup is a team competition in which players represent their countries and compete in an elimination format throughout the year.

In 2019, the Spanish team reached the final of the competition, where they faced Canada.

During the Davis Cup celebration in Madrid in November of that year, Rafa Nadal received news that his father, Sebastián Nadal, had passed away in Mallorca.

In this situation, the tennis player decided to skip the quarterfinals and semifinals of the competition to be with his family in those difficult times.

However, Rafa decided to come back to play the final against Canada.

In the first individual match of the final, Nadal faced Denis Shapovalov and achieved a crucial victory for the Spanish team.

Despite the pain of losing his father, Nadal managed to maintain the concentration and composure necessary to contribute to the final victory of his team.

90

Unbelievably, Roberto Bautista reported receiving death threats after losing the semi-finals of the Gstaad tournament to Fognini.

The Spaniard's social media was flooded with insults and threats to him and his family.

According to what he said hours later, they came from sports betting.

"Unfortunately, the world of sport is getting sullied through betting. What you have to put up with after having given everything," Bautista lamented on his Twitter profile.

91

In the 1920s, women's tennis began to gain popularity, but female tennis players were treated unequally compared to men.

In 1926, the first major women's tennis event, the French International Championship (now known as Roland Garros), was established, but it only allowed amateur women to participate.

In 1927, the United States Tennis Association decided to ban women from competing professionally in the tournaments it organized.

This ban was in effect for 14 years, preventing the development of professional women's tennis.

In 1941, the Women's Tennis Association (WTA) was founded, but World War II prevented major tournaments from taking place for several years.

In 1947, the WTA organized a series of exhibition matches between the world's top female tennis players, which helped revive interest in women's tennis.

Finally, in 1968, the Open Era of tennis began, allowing professional male and female players to compete together in Grand Slam tournaments.

This was a crucial moment in the history of women's tennis, and players like Billie Jean King, Margaret Court, and Chris Evert helped establish the WTA as a leading organization in the sport.

92

Why are tennis balls changed during matches?

The first change comes after playing the first seven games, and then every nine games.

This is because during warm-up, it is considered that the balls suffer wear equivalent to what would be two games.

Therefore, the end of their life is brought forward.

From the first change on, it is every nine games when ball kids open new cans.

The main goal is that, from a certain wear, the trajectory or bounces of the balls may have defects and harm the game.

In addition, the pressure begins to decrease, causing a lower bounce.

This is the explanation of why tennis balls are changed during matches, something that many people are unaware of and that is common in the white sport.

93

The tennis ball is usually only in play for about 20 minutes in a tennis match that lasts approximately two and a half hours.

This is because after each point, players have a few seconds to rest, change sides, and prepare for the next point.

Additionally, every time a point is played, the ball can go out of the court, which means it needs to be retrieved and prepared for the next point.

The amount of time the ball is in play can vary depending on factors such as the court surface, players' game strategy, and other factors, but it is generally estimated that the ball is in play around 10-15% of the total time of the match.

Therefore, although players may seem like they are not doing much during a tennis match, the amount of physical and mental effort required to play well is extremely high.

94

Around 325 million tennis balls are manufactured worldwide every year, contributing to around 22,000 tons of rubber waste.

The practice of recycling tennis and paddle balls is relatively new compared to other products or materials.

Nevertheless, it has gained ground in countries such as Canada, the United States, France, and Spain.

Currently, individuals and organizations committed to this cause have developed ways to integrate unused balls into a circular economy.

95

There is no definitive conclusion as to why "love" is used to represent "zero" in tennis.

The most commonly accepted theory is that the term "love" to represent a score of zero in tennis comes from Old French "l'oeuf," which means egg.

The reason behind this is that the shape of a zero resembles that of an egg, and the French used the word "l'oeuf" to refer to a zero in counting.

Over time, it is believed that the pronunciation of "l'oeuf" corrupted into "love," and the term was used in tennis and spread to other sports as well.

Another theory suggests that "love" comes from the English word "lof," which means "nothing" or "worthless."

However, the Old French theory is the most accepted by most sources.

96

Brad Parks and Jeff Minnenbraker are considered the pioneers of wheelchair tennis.

After his accident, Parks began playing tennis in a wheelchair to stay active and found in this sport a form of rehabilitation.

In 1976, he founded the National Wheelchair Tennis Association (NWTA) and organized the first official wheelchair tennis tournament in Los Angeles.

Wheelchair tennis has become an increasingly popular sport and has been included in the Paralympic Games since 1992.

It is played according to the same rules as conventional tennis, but players are allowed to bounce the ball twice before hitting it.

97

Paul Annacone is an American tennis coach who has worked with some of the world's top tennis players.

Born in 1963 in Southampton, New York, Annacone had a professional tennis career that spanned from the late 1970s to the early 1990s.

During that time, he won three doubles titles in Grand Slam tournaments.

After retiring as a player, Annacone became a coach and worked with several notable players, including Tim Henman, Sloane Stephens, and Roger Federer.

Annacone was Federer's head coach from mid-2010 until 2013, a period in which Federer regained the world number one ranking after an injury.

Annacone has also worked as a tennis commentator on television and has written several books about the sport, including "The Champion's Mind: How Great Athletes Think, Train, and Thrive" and "Coaching Tennis Successfully".

He is considered one of the world's top tennis coaches, especially in the area of serving and volleying, and has been inducted into the US Tennis Hall of Fame.

98

James Van Alen, a member of a wealthy New York family and a high-level tennis player, is known for his role in introducing the tie-break in tennis.

Van Alen was frustrated with the length of tennis matches, which often lasted for hours because players needed to win by two games in sets.

In 1965, Van Alen devised a tie-break system for tennis that would allow players to finish sets more quickly.

He proposed two types of tie-breaks: the first, known as "sudden-death tie-break", would end after a player reached nine points; and the second, the "persistent-death unbalance", would require a player to win by a two-point margin after reaching 12 points.

The idea was well-received by the tennis community, and after some successful trials, the tie-break was officially adopted at the US Open in 1970.

Since then, it has become an integral part of tennis gameplay worldwide and has helped to reduce the length of matches.

99

Hazel Hotchkiss Wightman is considered one of the first stars of women's tennis in the United States.

Born in 1886, she started playing tennis at the age of 12 and won her first national title in both singles and doubles in 1909.

Throughout her career, she won a total of 45 national championships, both in singles and doubles.

Wightman was a pioneer in the use of volley play and net approaches in women's tennis, earning her the nickname "Queen Mother of Tennis."

She was also one of the founders of the Wightman Cup, an international women's tennis competition between the United States and Great Britain that has been contested since 1923.

In addition to her success in tennis, Wightman was a leader in the tennis and sports community.

She was the first woman to serve on the board of directors of the United States Tennis Association (USTA) and founded the USTA Women's Committee in 1916.

She was also an advocate for gender equality in sports and worked to ensure that women had the same opportunities as men in tennis and other sports.

100

Promoter CC Pyle created the first professional tennis tour in 1926, with a group of American and French players playing exhibition matches for paying audiences.

The most notable of these early players were American Vinnie Richards and French woman Suzanne Lenglen.

Once a player turned professional, they could not compete in the major (amateur) tournaments.

In 1968, commercial pressures and rumours that some amateurs were taking money under the table led to the abandonment of this distinction, ushering in what is now known as the Open Era, in which players would compete in all tournaments, with the best able to make a living from the sport.

With the beginning of the Open Era, the establishment of an international professional tennis circuit and revenues from the sale of television rights, the popularity of tennis spread around the world.

Today, the sport has lost its English-speaking, middle- and upper-class image, although the stereotype still exists.

101

"Tennis for Two" is considered the first tennis video game in history.

It was created by American physicist William Higinbotham in 1958, as a demonstration for an annual visit event at Brookhaven National Laboratory in New York.

The game consisted of two points of light representing the rackets and a line in the middle representing the net.

Players could turn a knob to move the racket and hit the virtual ball. The screen displayed the trajectory of the ball and the score.

Although the game was only a demonstration, it is considered an important milestone in the history of video games and laid the foundation for many later tennis games.

Since then, numerous tennis games have been created for different platforms, including video game consoles, PC, and mobile devices.

If you have enjoyed the tennis curiosities presented in this book, we would like to ask you to share a review on Amazon.

Your opinion is extremely valuable to us and to other tennis enthusiasts who are looking to be entertained and learn new knowledge about this sport.

We understand that leaving a comment can be a tedious process, but we ask that you take a few minutes of your time to share your thoughts and opinions with us.

Your support is very important to us and helps us continue creating quality content for lovers of this amazing sport.

We appreciate your support in advance and wish you great success in your tennis matches.

May your shots be precise and your game be unstoppable!

★ ★ ★ ★ ★

Printed in Great Britain
by Amazon